A REPORT ON THE PROPOSED

ALLAGASH NATIONAL RIVERWAY

prepared by the

Bureau of Outdoor Recreation
United States Department of the Interior

July 1963

TABLE OF CONTENTS

INTRODUCTION   1

SUMMARY OF FINDINGS   4

SUMMARY OF RECOMMENDATIONS   8

FINDINGS   11
    Allagash River as a Recreation Resource   11
    Allagash River as a Free-Flowing Stream   12
    The Pattern of Land Use   12
    Existing Development and Use of Land and Resources   18
    Related Regional Recreation Resources   21
    Private, State, and Federal Proposals   22
    Support for Preservation of the Allagash   24

RECOMMENDATIONS   26
    Establishment of a National Riverway   26
    The Area and Its Administration   26
    Scenic Easement Zone   28
    Criteria for Boundary Selection   28
    Resource Management Principles   32
    Development and Use   34
    Estimate of Cost   37

APPENDIXES
    A Allagash River Authority Act
    B Recreation Advisory Council--Relationship of
          Allagash to Council Policy Circular No. 1
    C Map - Land Use and Boundary Proposal
    D Map - Land Ownership

ILLUSTRATIONS

1   The Allagash River as it exists today   3

2   Canoeing the Allagash   10

3   The Allagash River is primarily a water-   16
        oriented primitive river canoeing area

4   Canoeists beach their craft to rearrange   19
        cargo prior to running Chase Rapids

5   Allagash Falls   38

6   Portage around Allagash Falls   39

INTRODUCTION

In June of 1962 the Secretary of the Interior, in a memorandum to the Director, Bureau of Outdoor Recreation, discussed the need for formulating a sound policy of resource development in the upper St. John River area of Maine, including the advisability of hydro-electric power development on the upper St. John River and the protection of the unusual natural recreation aspects associated with the Allagash River. He specifically requested recommendations as to the best overall approach to the protection and utilization of the recreation resources in the Allagash area.

The Secretary, in a report of July 1, 1963, to the President, recommending the early authorization of the International Passamaquoddy Tidal Project and the upper St. John River hydro-electric power development, noted that the "proposed plan would preserve in its entirety the free flowing nature of the Allagash River and its superb recreational values."

The Secretary of the Interior and the Secretary of Agriculture jointly directed a cooperative effort by the Department of the Interior and the Department of Agriculture under the leadership of the Director, Bureau of Outdoor Recreation to study and recommend adequate protection for the Nation's remaining wild rivers where opportunities for such protection still remain. This action was taken on May 14, 1963, sometime subsequent to the specific instructions to the Bureau of Outdoor Recreation for a study of the Allagash River.

This report considers the Allagash River as only one of the Nation's free flowing streams suitable for protection by the Federal government.

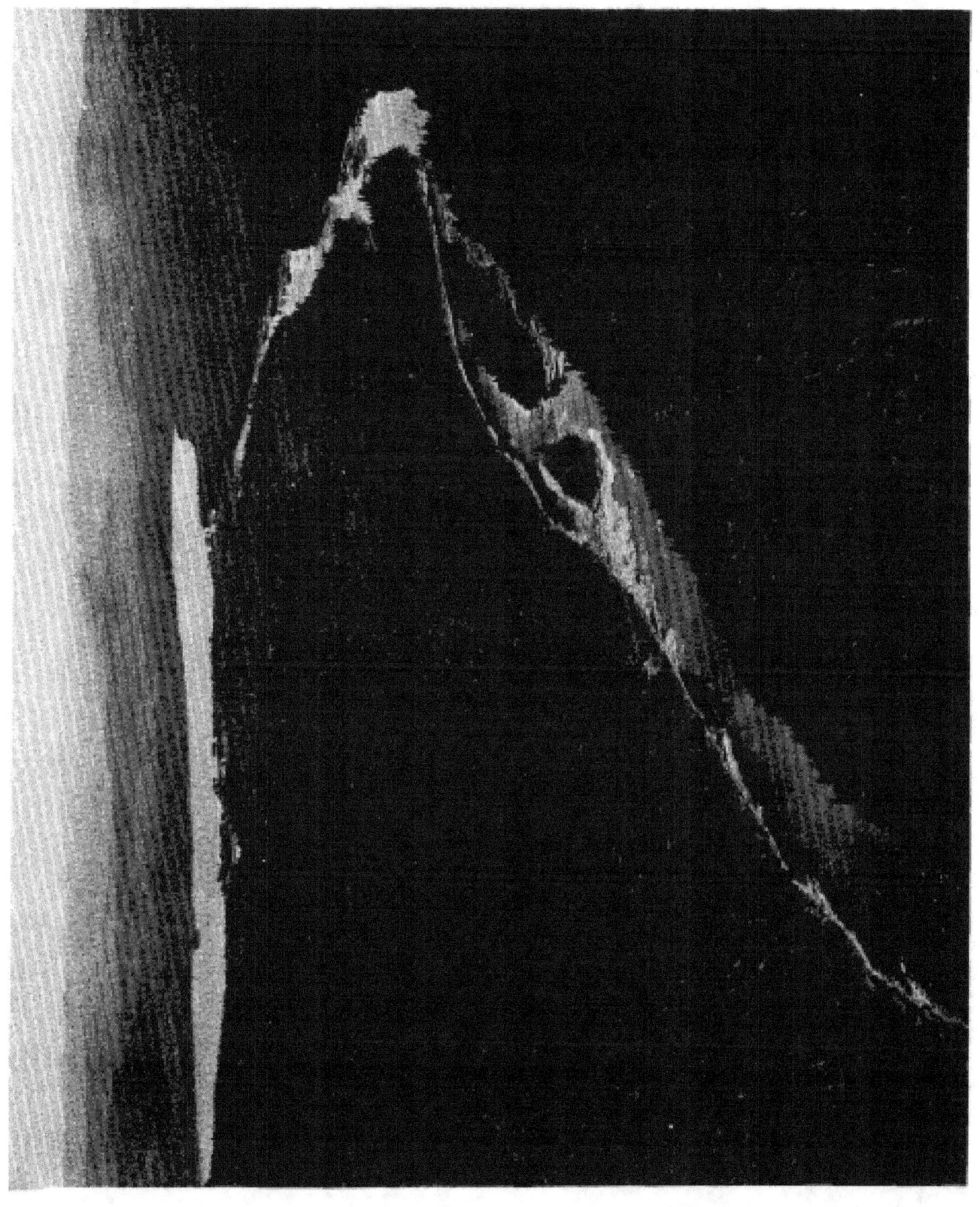

National Park Service

Illus. 1. The Allagash River as it exists today.

SUMMARY

FINDINGS   The Allagash River, located in the backwoods of northern

Maine, is one of the few remaining free-flowing streams

of importance in the eastern United States. It is a major recreation

resource of great potential significance to the Nation.

Throughout the country, water resources are being extensively

developed and utilized. Many natural rivers already have been

irrevocably committed to uses which leave little room for the funda-

mental pleasures associated with the natural environment. In view

of this trend, wild and semi-wild rivers such as the Allagash become

increasingly important from the standpoint of retention for present

use, as well as comparable use by future generations.

If the Allagash is not preserved, it will mean that the Nation

has lost access to an adventuresome outdoor experience which it has

treasured since early times.

With proper safeguards, the Allagash offers an opportunity to

preserve an important segment of our national heritage. Without

safeguards, the Allagash River and its environs may be used

increasingly for industrial purposes.

4

The purpose of an Allagash National Riverway would be to insure an area in the eastern United States of sufficient size and quality where present and future generations may experience a primitive northwoods canoeing adventure.

To achieve this purpose, it is necessary to preserve the natural free-flowing character of the river; maintain the quality and quantity of its waters; and keep the primitive northwoods character of its surroundings.

Although isolated by nature, the Allagash offers a richly-rewarding experience to visitors willing to expend the effort to explore the area. In this land of primitive river travel, they find a superb environment and reap the lasting satisfaction of enjoying a form of recreation gradually disappearing from the national scene.

The Allagash River drains a watershed which for more than one hundred years has been dedicated to the growth and harvest of timber. Since wood resources are of importance to the area, the final plan designed to protect the unique recreation resources should allow harvesting of the timber resources except immediately adjacent to the waterways.

With the exception of the great ponds and school lots in each township, all of the 1.8 million acres which comprise the Allagash region are privately owned. The principal landholders of the area that constitutes the Allagash waterways are Great Northern Paper Company, International Paper Company, and the Wheatland interests.

These lands are currently used for multiple purposes, but the emphasis
is placed on timber and its use for lumber and pulpwood.

Maine is world-renowned for its scenic beauty, forests, seacoasts,
waterways, and other exceptional natural wonders, as well as unusually
fine facilities for recreation and sport. On innumerable lakes and
rivers, the State and private interests have provided for and encouraged intensive recreation use. There is no dearth of opportunity for
those persons desiring to take advantage of water-oriented activities,
including swimming, water skiing, sailing, and power boating.

Dedication of the Allagash National Riverway to a less intensive
type of recreation will not adversely affect the recreation habits
of Maine's citizens or the host of out-of-state visitors who seek
pleasure in the State each year. Preserving the Allagash in its free-
flowing state--and thus perpetuating a primitive recreation experience--
will simply strengthen the image of a State already famous for its
northwoods atmosphere and rugged features.

Primitive water travel should take precedent over all other uses
of the Allagash. The area is not suited for intensive, concentrated
use. Travel and camping along portions of the river and lakes of
the Allagash would offer an exhilarating experience to those seeking
a primitive environment.

Recreation activities that are compatible with the traditional
canoe trip are: fishing for native brook trout and togue, hunting
for deer, bear and waterfowl, and hiking along or near the waterways
that offer excellent opportunities for a natural history experience.

Thus, the water, forests, and wildlife through use become the recreation resources of this region. The recreation needs associated with remoteness, the opportunity to know nature intimately, and the opportunity to lose oneself in time rather than distance greatly enhance the value and usefulness of these resources. These are conditions that now exist on much of the watershed. They can be maintained only if intensive use is excluded.

Establishment of a National Riverway in the region would give recognition to the fact that few such semi-wild areas still are available. It would mean attainment of an objective sorely needed to help satisfy present and future recreation needs of the Nation.

The alternative to public protection and preservation of the area, which could be under Federal, State, or joint Federal-State administration, is to leave it with private commercial interests. Such a decision offers no real assurance to the public that the river, lakes, and natural environment of the Allagash will not eventually be encroached upon by diverse industrial demands.

Support for protection and preservation of certain of the Nation's free-flowing streams has been widely expressed by Federal and State conservation agencies, private organizations, the Outdoor Recreation Resources Review Commission, and the Senate Select Committee on National Water Resources.

SUMMARY OF
RECOMMENDATIONS   To preserve the Allagash River in its free

                         flowing state and natural setting it is

recommended that:

1. An Allagash National Riverway be established in northern
Maine by act of Congress.

2. The Riverway encompass the principal waterway travel routes
typically adapted to canoes and considered to have significant primitive
recreation qualities and important to overall preservation objectives.

3. The boundary of the Riverway be authorized to be fixed at
not more than one half a mile from the principal waterway travel routes
as delineated on Map BOR-ANR-1000, Appendix C, and be finally determined
following authorization of the Riverway by the Congress.

4. The Riverway be managed primarily for primitive canoe travel
and associated activities such as camping, fishing, hunting, and other
recreation activities compatible with the primitive environment. This
would preclude the use of motors on boats and of airplanes equipped
with either floats or skis.

5. All private land and water within the Riverway be acquired
in fee either by acquisition or by donation. Owners of improved
property should be allowed to reserve the right of use and occupancy
for non-commercial residential purposes for 25 years. Owners of
commercial properties should not be permitted to reserve any right
of use or occupancy for commercial purposes.

6. The State of Maine be permitted to reserve its lands and great
ponds or deed them to the Federal government. If the State of Maine

wishes to reserve its right to the great ponds (water areas over 10 acres), the right to control the use of the water on the great ponds should be vested in the Federal government.

7. Flowage rights now in existence by reason of an act of the Maine legislature be extinguished.

8. The State of Maine be invited to assist in the administration of fish and game matters and in the protection of vegetation from fire, insect, and diseases.

9. Public access to the Riverway be provided only at points near Telos Lake, Umsaskis Lake-Long Lake, and Allagash Falls. The development of private supporting facilities for canoe rental, supplies, and equipment may be provided at these public access points.

10. Permanent overnight visitor accommodations, if required, be developed outside the Riverway.

11. The National Park Service be designated to administer the Riverway.

12. The Allagash National Riverway Act authorize the acquisition of scenic easements up to one half a mile from the finally established boundary of the Riverway for the purpose of protecting the scenic aspects of the land as viewed from the water course. Such easements would not affect the sustained-yield capacity of the forest lands but simply provide for the cooperative planning of timber harvesting in such a way as to minimize the effect of such harvesting as related to the view from the water.

Maine Forest Service

Illus. 2. Canoeing the Allagash

FINDINGS

ALLAGASH RIVER AS A
RECREATION RESOURCE

Located deep in the backwoods of Maine, the Allagash River flows northward for nearly 100 miles through forests of spruce-fir, maple, and birch. Linked by quiet lakes of tranquil beauty, the Allagash River has long been hailed by outdoor enthusiasts as one of the major primitive river courses in the United States. A traditional canoe trip on the Allagash is regarded as a classic canoeing experience by many who have made the journey.

In a discussion of the recreation resources of the Allagash region, it must be noted that the primeval structure has been altered by timber-cutting, by construction of access roads, by man-made dams, and by sheer recreation use. But, it is of equal importance to note that the river, its tributaries, and lakes remain relatively undisturbed.

One of the important differences between rivers and most other outdoor recreation land resources lies in the linear characteristic of the former. Recreation in a wilderness area depends on the entire area. This means the flora, fauna, topography, lakes, streams, and the very air of the area. A river is a primary part of the environment as well as a line of access.

The means of travel on the Allagash waterways is the principal attraction. Keeping the waterways undisturbed offers a challenge and fascination to those inclined toward a mode of travel that demands skill and dexterity to overcome unordinary hazards. Such are the recreation qualities of an area that should be protected against the gradual encroachment of an expanding civilization.

ALLAGASH RIVER AS A   Only in recent years has recognition been
FREE-FLOWING STREAM
                             given to the importance of preserving some
of the Nation's streams and lakes for recreation uses.

Because industrial pollution or impoundment can easily impair or destroy the recreation quality of streams, many individuals, State Governments, and Federal agencies, have expressed a strong interest in a nationwide classification of streams.

The Outdoor Recreation Resources Review Commission report recommended that certain rivers be preserved in their free-flowing state and natural setting. Such streams are the ones with natural attributes which, in their total effect, are so unique as to warrant permanent preservation.

Artificial impoundment cannot satisfy the type of recreation demand offered by such unusual waterways. The Allagash River, with its fine natural environment and isolated qualities, admirably qualifies as a free-flowing stream worthy of preservation.

THE PATTERN   1. Land Ownership. Ownership of the Allagash
OF LAND USE
                     area is divided among two groups: Pulp and paper
companies which depend upon their Allagash holdings to varying degrees

for raw material supplies; and private individuals or groups who sell available timber for stumpage.

In addition to privately-owned lands, public lots totalling 1000 acres exist in each unorganized township. Since a majority of the townships have not been surveyed, it is not possible at this time to pinpoint the location of these public areas.

Of the public lots located, it was found that in most instances, grass and timber rights have been sold to pulp and paper companies. Great ponds (any lake in excess of 10 acres) are owned by the State of Maine.

The two largest landholding companies in the entire Allagash region are Great Northern Paper Company and International Paper Company. These two companies own approximately 50 percent of the region's acreage of some 1.8 million acres. The seven largest landholders--four paper companies and three family interests--own more than 80 percent of the acreage in the locality.

The concentration of land ownership in the proposed National River-way is similar to that found in the Allagash region as a whole, and is divided among Great Northern Paper Company, International Paper Company, and the Wheatland interests. In addition to the principal land holders and the State of Maine, the following companies and individuals own varying amounts of land within the area:

John Cassidy Estate, Penobscot Development Company, Irving Pulp and Paper Company, Griswald heirs, Heron Lake Dam Company, East Branch

Improvement Company, St. John Sulphite, Ltd., William J. Durst, Lester
M. Farrington, Abraham Leibowitz, and Henry Taylor. There are a number
of lots that have been leased to various individuals by the property
owners. Sporting camps and summer cottages have been built on a number
of these lots. (See Land Ownership Map, data as of 1961, Appendix D).

2. <u>Land Management</u>. Most of the lands in the Allagash Region are
managed on a sustained forest yield basis to give both current income
and capital growth. These lands currently are used for multiple purposes,
with the management practices predominantly aligned toward the timber
resource and its use for lumber and pulpwood.

Cutting rates in the region have varied over the years and have
been estimated at about 60-70 percent of the annual growth rate. However, there have been predictions by several of the companies that in
the next few years cuts will nearly equal the growth rates.

At present, the cutting cycle is determined primarily by the
species composition of the stands; usually only mature timber is cut.
Spruce and fir are cut on a cycle of twenty to forty years. The
cutting cycle of hardwoods varies with market conditions, and cedar
and pine are harvested at irregular intervals.

As a result of changes in production techniques, timber formerly
cut in this watershed and floated out by water is now hauled out by
truck. While the development of an extensive road system in this area
has allowed greatly increased timber harvest, it also poses the
greatest single threat to the primitive character of the Allagash.

An important feature of the National Riverway proposal is its recognition of the desirability of continuing timber harvesting in most of the region to meet the needs of the companies operating in the Allagash.

    3. <u>Recreation Use</u>. By its very nature, the Allagash is isolated. A conclusion of the Outdoor Recreation Resources Review Commission Study Report on "Wilderness and Recreation" was that the relative inaccessibility of an area does not prevent its being utilized. The report indicated that the more distinctive an area is, the more willing people are to travel long distances to utilize it. For instance, 56 percent of the persons visiting the Boundary Waters Canoe Area in Minnesota traveled as far as 500 miles for a wilderness river-lake experience.

While it is true that the Allagash region has not been an important contributor in the past to the total recreation picture of the State or Nation, it nevertheless is influenced by the same use pressures found in similar areas elsewhere. Its future role is directly related to the growth of recreation in this country and Canada. It is well documented that since World War II, outdoor recreation in the Nation's forests and parks has increased tremendously. The trend promises to continue.

Recreation use of the Allagash region has been increasing gradually and can be expected to intensify. To illustrate, in the period 1958-1960 the total number of through parties making the traditional canoe trip down the Allagash River nearly doubled. A river count conducted from mid-June to mid-October, 1962, revealed that over 1000 persons

15

Maine Forest Service

Illus. 3. The Allagash River is primarily a water-oriented primitive river canoeing area.

traveled the river. In addition, a substantial number of recreationists used other portions of the lakes and river above the check point located near Allagash Falls and thus were not counted.

There is also ample evidence that in addition to increased canoe travel in recent years, the region is being utilized heavily as a general recreation area by campers, hunting and fishing parties, power boat enthusiasts, and others. There is a constantly growing air plane traffic to and from all portions of the area that afford water surface adequate for landing and taking off. This activity is most pronounced in the summer. In addition, an increasing number of people fly in to take advantage of the excellent ice fishing during the winter months.

Visitation at nearby Baxter State Park for the 1962 season was estimated at 61,500 persons. Of this number, 18,590 camped out in primitive shelters or otherwise took advantage of the backwoods environment. The remaining number drove through the area for sightseeing purposes. From the foregoing it is readily discernible that the region is utilized four seasons of the year.

Although the growth and harvest of timber are the dominant land uses in the Allagash watershed, landowners have taken note of the growing demand for recreation throughout the region. Accordingly, this activity has been assigned a position in the management plans of the landholding interests. In cooperation with the Maine Forest Service, primitive campsites have been developed, and many miles of logging roads heretofore closed to the public are now open to travel. The extent of

17

this involvement in recreation matters is, of course, secondary to the primary functions of the Maine Forest Service and landowners. Neither the State agency nor the landowner has a mandate to devote any appreciable time or effort to developing or protecting recreation resources for public benefit. Consequently, there are acknowledged difficulties and a lack of coordinated effort in providing adequate maintenance and protection standards at many of the more popular lakeshore areas.

The recreation carrying capacity of the waterways and the effect its use will generate on the shoreline and other environmental features will determine future use of the Allagash National Riverway. Studies to determine the recreation carrying capacity are essential to ensure that the enjoyment of future users will not be jeopardized by severe overcrowding that would bring about deterioration and eventual destruction of the area's unique features and atmosphere.

To provide protection and a buffer zone for the waterways, and to allow for a balanced recreation use of the resource, it will be necessary to acquire private lands and flowage rights, along with publicly owned lands and water rights in the area.

EXISTING DEVELOPMENT AND USE OF LAND AND RESOURCES

In spite of the best intentions and desires of many people, the distinguishing characteristics associated with the Allagash waterways gradually are slipping away.

During the brief span of 10 years, an expanding network of private gravel and dirt roads has penetrated deeper into the area.

Maine Forest Service

Illus. 4. Canoeists beach their craft to rearrange cargo prior to running Chase Rapids

A scattering of sporting camps and private cottages emphasizes the mounting pressures from persons seeking lakeshore lots for vacation purposes. Recreation use associated with power boating has swept over lakes accessible by road. Gaining momentum is the one-day-or-less float plane fishing or hunting excursion.

The expanding road system presents the most serious threat to the preservation of the waterways. From the south, a road to Telos Lake is open to the public. To the east, a road from Ashland, Maine, bisects the waterways at the Long Lake-Umsaskis Lake thoroughfare. This road continues on to Clayton Lake and from there extends into Canada. Field headquarters for the International Paper Company are located at Clayton Lake. Side roads penetrate to Cunliffe Lake, Priestly Lake, and Churchill Lake. These roads are open to the public by special permission from the paper companies.

Logging roads from the Musquacook Lakes skirt the periphery of Clear Lake, Twin Lake, Spider Lake, Cliff Lake, and Haymock Lake. A logging road traverses the arm of Chamberlain Lake, crosses the Round Pond thoroughfare, and dead ends near Umbazooksus Lake. This is one of several water crossings maintained and used by the Great Northern Paper Company. A representative number of these roads and water crossings have been identified on the maps attached to this report as Appendix C and D.

Further down the Allagash River, a good road parallels the west bank. Its origin is at the mouth of the Allagash, and it pushes several miles upstream beyond Michaud Farm. This road is used extensively by the public for convenient access to the river and as a departure and return point for trips into the interior lakes.

All of these roads are maintained in a manner to facilitate the movement of the timber product by modern methods of transportation. One company estimates its road investment in the proposed area as $440,000.

It is the spirit and intent of the National Riverway proposal to limit road building within the area. Only those roads necessary for public or administrative access would be authorized. Furthermore such roads as now exist and found non-essential for public access or administrative use should be obliterated.

The intrusions by roads and other means have modified the physical features and the character and quality of the recreation opportunities. Even so, the Allagash is not yet lost as a primitive river canoe country. What has been done could be undone, and the waterways with their attending environment can still be retained for the enjoyment of future generations.

The manner by which this could most judiciously be accomplished is set forth in the following portions of this report.

RELATED REGIONAL RECREATION RESOURCES East through Telos Lake, and connected to the Allagash Watershed by small Webster Lake, lies the Mt. Katahdin country of Baxter State Park. Katahdin with its sheer, glistening walls and glacial cirques enclosing high-lying ponds also symbolizes the very best of the Maine wilderness.

The Allagash River, its lakes, and tributaries are a worthy complement to the existing mountain wilderness preserve of Baxter State Park, which lies only 15 miles from Telos Lake.

These two distinct types of recreation areas would be complimented by the power boating and related recreation opportunities afforded by the proposed Dickey impoundment on the St. John River.

PRIVATE,STATE,AND
FEDERAL PROPOSALS

1. State Agencies. A bill to create an Allagash River Authority for the State of Maine was introduced in the 1963 session of the Maine State Legislature and enacted into law on June 27, 1963. It declares that the policy of the State of Maine is "to provide for the preservation of the natural beauty and the wilderness character of the Allagash River Watercourse while utilizing the natural economic resources of the watercourse." The law provides for the creation of the Allagash River Authority consisting of five members whose duties would be to formulate plans and proposals for preserving the watercourse. It authorizes the Authority to enter into tentative agreements with the land owners with respect to lands, interest in land, leases, cooperative agreements, agreements, and development rights, looking forward to carrying out the expressed policy of the State of Maine. Such plans and proposals as the Authority may recommend are subject to the final approval of the next Legislature of the State of Maine.

The law as enacted may be considered as planning authority and not authority to proceed with the actual setting aside of lands through purchase or agreement for the purpose of preserving the free flowing qualities of the Allagash River and its tributaries. A copy of the act is set forth in Appendix A.

2. _Private Sector._ The current _policy_ of the landowners is to protect the recreation values in such a manner that Federal or State action is unnecessary. However, this policy can give no assurance that it will be continued, or that it will offer the protection that a public agency dedicated to conserving recreation resources can offer. Like all policies not defined by law, it is neither more nor less than a decision on the part of forest landowners and can be revoked at will.

3. _Federal Proposals._ The National Park Service in a published report issued in June of 1961 proposed the Allagash National Recreation Area which would have comprised 246,500 acres of forest land and 50,000 acres of water surface. In contrast, the Allagash National Riverway proposal would authorize a maximum area of 154,000 acres of forest land and 38,000 acres of water surface. The actual acquisition of forest land should be considerably less than the 154,000 acres.

The National Park Service proposal included the Musquacook chain of lakes. The national riverway proposal eliminates this chain.

The National Park Service proposal would have authorized hunting only on certain portions of the national recreation area. The national riverway proposal will permit hunting throughout the area with temporary restrictions only in cases of need for public safety or for wildlife management purposes.

SUPPORT FOR PRESERVA-
TION OF THE ALLAGASH
The undisturbed character of the water-

ways and the natural environment through

which this river flows set the Allagash apart from other attractive

resort and natural areas in the eastern part of the United States.

Specific support for reserving an unspoiled area representative

of the Northern Maine uplands has been expressed by the following

organizations:

1. New England-New York Interagency Committee. The studies

carried out by this committee in 1953-55 recognized, and recommended

the preservation of, certain outstanding scenic and recreation

attractions of the St. John River Basin. The Allagash River was

identified as possessing unique opportunities for canoeing, camping,

fishing, hunting, and vacationing in a wilderness setting.

2. State Park Commission, Maine. In 1956, the State Park Com-

mission published its recreation and parks program. The report stated

that preservation of the Allagash River was important. Since the

issuance of that report, the Commission members have decided that they

have received no new information that would change the position taken

in 1956.

3. Bureau of Sport Fisheries and Wildlife. One of the Bureau's

principal recommendations in a report dated October 1, 1959, regarding

the Rankin Rapids project on the upper St. John River was that the

Allagash River and adequate adjoining lands be maintained for wilderness-

type recreation use. The report further states that fish and wildlife

resources of outstanding value would be destroyed by construction of the

Rankin Rapids project.

4. Maine Department of Inland Fisheries and Game. In March, 1960, this Department went on record as opposing the Rankin Rapids project and favoring the alternate Big Rapids-Lincoln School project as one much less damaging to the fish and wildlife resources of this area.

5. Senate Select Committee on Natural Resources. In early 1961, the Committee recommended "that certain streams be preserved in their free-flowing condition because their natural scenic, scientific, esthetic, and recreation values outweigh their values for water development and control purposes now and in the future." The Select Committee report suggests several rivers that meet these requirements: the Allagash River in Maine, the Current and Eleven Point Rivers in Missouri, and the Rogue River in Oregon.

6. National Park Service. In July 1961, the Service proposed that a territory embracing most of the river course and tributary lakes be set aside as an Allagash National Recreation Area for wilderness recreation.

7. Natural Resources Council of Maine. In its August 1962 bulletin, Proposals for the Allagash, the Council recommended land acquisition and management by State or Federal government that would assure complete protection for the Allagash River course.

RECOMMENDATIONS

ESTABLISHMENT OF A
NATIONAL RIVERWAY
It is recommended that an Allagash National Riverway be established in Northern Maine by Act of Congress. Establishment of the project would conform to the criteria for National Recreation Areas as defined by the President's Recreation Advisory Council. (See Appendix B - Relationship of Allagash National Riverway to Council Policy Circular No. 1).

THE AREA AND ITS
ADMINISTRATION
The Department of the Interior should acquire and administer the area. It would be advantageous for the Department to rely on the State of Maine for assistance in the administration and protection of the timber and wildlife resources found within the proposed Riverway. The State has long been active in fire, insect, and disease control and in the regulation of hunting and fishing. Accordingly, it is recommended that the Department utilize the assistance of the State of Maine for these purposes.

It is recommended that the actual boundary of the Riverway be fixed following an intensive survey after an authorizing act has been passed. Such boundary should be fixed at not further than one half a mile from the water as shown on the schematic map entitled "A Proposed Allagash National Riverway" and appended hereto as Appendix C.

This boundary should encompass the principal waterway travel routes typically adaptable to canoes and considered to have significant primitive recreation qualities and important to overall preservation objectives.

The principal waterways and a strip of land not to exceed one half a mile from these waterways would then comprise the Allagash National Riverway and is recommended for Federal ownership and administration. This land area and the ponds under 10 acres in extent should be acquired by purchase or donation. Ponds over 10 acres which are presently owned by the State of Maine might be acquired by donation or purchase. However, this is not necessary if the State will cede jurisdiction over the use and control of the water to the Federal government. Approximately 38,000 acres are involved in the great ponds included within the proposed Riverway.

It is recommended that the flowage rights of the Heron Lake Dam Company be closed out. This may be accomplished through action by the State Legislature. These flowage rights permit their owner to construct a dam and to change water levels without regard to the free flowing stream objectives of the waterway proposal.

The boundary for the riverway, as shown on the accompanying schematic map is labelled "Proposed Maximum Limit of National Riverway." This boundary is not recommended for adoption. It is recommended only in the sense that the precise boundary shall not extend more than one half a mile from the waterways.

27

SCENIC EASE-
MENT ZONE
It is further recommended that the enabling
legislation authorize the Secretary of the
Interior to negotiate with the land owners for   scenic easements
covering lands not to extend more than one half a mile beyond the
final boundary for the Allagash Riverway. Under a scenic easement
the owner of the land continues to own it and use it but, for an agreed
upon fee, relinquishes his right to modify the existing use of the
land. The scenic easement would permit the continued harvest of the
timber. It would contemplate cooperative planning between the Secretary
of the Interior and the land owner in programming the harvesting of
the timber so as to maximize the scenic aspects of the harvested area
as viewed from the watercourse. Land owners would continue to follow
their own policy with respect to the use of their logging roads by
hunters and fishermen. They would continue to construct such physical
improvements as might be required in their timber operations. They
would be encouraged to continue their policy of discouraging the general
public,except hunters and fishermen, from the use of these lands.

CRITERIA FOR BOUNDARY
SELECTION
The boundaries were delineated on the
basis of the following criteria:

1. The need to include in the area the natural features considered
essential in maintaining the integrity of a free-flowing stream, thereby
insuring that present and future generations could continue to enjoy
primitive northwoods canoeing experiences in an eastern United States

area that affords sufficient size and quality. The suggested boundary excludes as much merchantable timber land as possible.

The application of this criterion involved consideration of preserving scenic features and waterways, providing for sufficient living space and access corridors, selecting a readily administrable boundary, and evaluating the potential value of scenic areas that have been disturbed by past action of man.

2. Extending the boundary inland as far as one half a mile from all shorelines was considered the maximum necessary to afford protection to the wilderness values of the watercourse. Some measure of the probable effectiveness of this recommendation may be obtained from a recent research observation of visitor reaction to timber harvest in the Boundary Water Canoe Area in Minnesota. In 1930 the Shipstead-Newton-Nolan law prohibited logging generally in a zone 400 feet back from navigable water bodies and near portages. A survey conducted in 1960 and 1961 disclosed that 92 percent of the canoeists travelling the waterways did not notice the logging operations. On the basis of this research study, it is possible to restrict the land zone of the proposed Allagash National Riverway to an area not less than 400 feet and not greater than 2,600 feet from the water's edge. The final boundary as selected following intensive surveys would probably be closer to 400 feet in width than to 2,600 feet.

There follow a review and discussion of the principal considerations that led to decisions on what to include and what not to include within the suggested boundary:

To assure permanent protection of the river, it is necessary to encompass certain lakes and tributary streams which are the reservoirs that supply the life blood needed to perpetuate the river flow.

The proposed Allagash National Riverway is primarily a water-oriented primitive river canoeing area. It then follows that the traditional canoeing approaches and portages long in use at Allagash Lake through Round Pond on the southwest, from Umbazooksus Lake to Mud Pond on the south, and at Webster Lake on the southeast should be protected and become an integral part of the proposed National Riverway.

To enhance the canoeing experience, it is desirable to include those tributary streams that provide the most significant variety of recreation experiences. These water courses, in addition to assuring water quantity in the river, contribute measurably in providing fishing, boating, and exploring satisfaction and help to set the scenic tone.

Smith Brook, draining Haymook Lake, is typical of a few of the Allagash tributaries that meet this criteria. Others similar to Smith Brook were included in their entirety if they were navigable the full length. Additional streams, particularly from Long Lake to Allagash Falls, while navigable only a short distance, do offer the opportunity for the canoeist to leave the river for a short time and explore new hunting or fishing areas, view beaver dams, or relax in the stillness of the northwoods.

While certain tributaries and lakes may appear insignificant when viewed from a map or the air, on the ground they become an essential segment of the river environment. This essential quality is typified by the fact that the numerous river tributaries include extensive spawning and nursery areas for trout. The Allagash Brook trout and other fish such as the native togue are maintained by natural repro- duction and migration from adjoining waters.

The Department of Inland Fisheries and Game substantiates the statement that the fishery resource in Eagle Lake, Long Lake, and Umsaskis Lake depends upon the many inlet tributaries that provide spawning grounds. Pillsbury Pond, Soper Pond, and Priestly Lake are valuable for this reason.

Lakes such as Haymock, Allagash, and Priestly are of importance because they are relatively unexploited and remain serene in their primitive environment.

Not to be forgotten are the important wildlife and waterfowl feed- ing areas at the mouth of Chemquosabamticook Stream and in the vicinity of the Musquacook dead waters. The suggested boundary enfolds these important environmental scenes that can be viewed as the canoeist trav- els the Allagash River. The opportunity to observe and enjoy wildlife adds pleasure to recreation activities.

This variety of scene is further enhanced by sites of historic and archeologic interest. These include sites of old Indian villages and evidence of historic lumbering days. Fortunately these areas are for the most part located close to the waterways and do not require an extension of boundary.

The suggested boundary does not include the Musquacook Lakes and greater portion of the stream or that portion of timber land lying between the Allagash River and the Musquacook Lakes area. The area comprising the Musquacook Lakes was excluded because it has already become subjected to public use pressures brought about by a public road from Ashland, Maine. For practical purposes, this road, the scattered developments already firmly entrenched along the lakeshores, and those which are planned irrevocably commit the area to uses incompatible with the primitive area objective of an Allagash National Riverway.

With the deletion of the Musquacook Lakes, there is not sufficient reason to include within the boundary of the proposed National Riverway that area lying between the lakes and the Allagash River. This mountainous area is heavily forested. There are no particular outstanding recreation benefits for canoeists, and these lands should remain available for multiple use.

RESOURCE MANAGE-
MENT PRINCIPLES
1. The National Riverway should be managed primarily for primitive river canoe travel. Its management objectives should serve to maintain the Allagash River as a free-flowing stream without impoundments, maintain the physical quality of the rivers, lakes, and tributaries and the water quantity

therein, and protect the natural environment along with the age-old quality of the recreation opportunities associated with these waterways.

2. Remove gradually man-made encroachments and prevent further intrusion of private and public roads and other uses and developments that are incompatible with the purpose of maintaining the primitive values immediately adjacent to the waterways. By reference to the schematic map attached as Appendix C, two situations may be identified wherein lands within scenic easement zones appear to have access blocked off by lands to be acquired in fee as part of the riverway. This may or may not actually be the case as the final boundary is yet to be determined. In any event, access to the scenic easement zone for timber harvesting will be provided.

3. Accord priority to policies, plans, improvements, and administrative acts that will facilitate and fortify recreation use of lands bordering the lakes and watercourses consistent with principles 1 and 2 above.

DEVELOPMENT   1. Detailed limitations on uses allowed in
AND USE
                      the proposed Riverway follow:

   Qualities characteristic of the area to be maintained. Recreation
use emphasizing primitive river canoe travel accorded dominant priority.
Cutting of timber not permitted. Hunting and fishing authorized in
accordance with State regulations. No permits issued for prospecting
or consent given for mineral leasing. No further alteration of water
below natural low water mark to be authorized. Occupancy in this zone
for administrative and recreation purposes only. Management aimed
at closing out the few privately owned resorts as rapidly as possible,
and permitting the continued use of existing private cottages for a
period of 25 years. Only those roads needed for administrative access
authorized. All other roads that penetrate this zone blocked and
obliterated. Campsites spaced at appropriate locations and accessible
only by water, with unpretentious campground structures, and signs, as
well as portages the only facilities provided. Float and ski planes
and motor boats permitted on the waterways only to service and facilitate riverway area management and protection. Canoe travel on waterways
by means imitative of the early voyagers. No access roads or trails
from water to scenic areas.

   There is common agreement that up to a certain point the number
of people who may see and enjoy a given area may be increased, but
beyond that point everybody would not have the same scene or enjoyment--

rather everybody may get less and more often nothing. This law of diminishing returns certainly applies at the Allagash. What is the expected use of the Allagash Riverway and at what point might the use become overuse?

For the purposes of this report an arbitrary rule of thumb has been taken to denote a contemplated maximum. Only research may ultimately determine the point of diminishing returns. If we assume as a maximum five two-man canoes for each lineal mile of the waterway and 100 miles of lineal waterways, 1,000 people could be on the water at any given time. Translating this into a 90-day season would give a tentative maximum annual capacity for the Allagash Riverway of 90,000 canoeists.

2. Suggested physical improvements within the Riverway:

Traditional canoe routes entering the Allagash watershed should continue as an important means of access. Once inside the area, since portages must be made, travel is possible only by canoes or other craft that the traveler can lift or carry. Limited hiking trips are possible over some of the old logging roads and fire trails, but extended foot travel would be difficult because of water and terrain. Horse travel would be permitted.

With careful planning, narrow scenic "corridors" that lead to the riverway from the surrounding lands could serve as the principal living space needed by individuals planning trips into the heartlands of the Allagash waterways. From these conventional gateways to the area's fringe, indoctrination of the traveler to the requirements of primitive river adventure can be carried out. These corridors would make use of existing roads leading to Telos Lake, Umsaskis Lake-Long Lake, and Allagash Falls.

While the majority of campsites would be accessible only by canoe, others would be accessible by road at the three principal access points named. Canoes can be launched and removed easily from the water at these locations.

At these three principal access points, canoe rental, supply and equipment rental, and guide and interpretive services could be provided. It is intended that visitors could carry and put up tents or other portable shelter. No permanent overnight visitor accommodations are planned for the area. If these are required, they should be developed outside the area.

It may be necessary to construct portages in some locations around rapids or low water.

Personnel assigned to the area would require certain facilities. These should be located where the public could best be served. The facilities would include utility, maintenance, and seasonal residences needed for park operation. The State of Maine has a number of fire lookouts on high points and a few fire-warden stations in the area. These should remain if required by the State of Maine. In all cases, necessary improvements should fit primitive area standards as closely as possible.

ESTIMATE
OF COST

If a National Riverway is established, it is estimated that the acquisition of private lands would cost approximately $4.6 million. This estimate is based on recent transactions in the area involving the sale of woodlands for $35 to $40 an acre.

The maximum forest acreage is estimated at 154,000 acres which at $40 an acre would total $6,160,000. However, it is estimated that not more than seventy-five percent of the maximum acreage will ultimately be required. Hence the estimated cost of acquisition would be reduced to $4.6 million. There has been no reliable figure developed for acquiring the scenic easements. The cost of acquiring the 30,000 acres of water surface (great ponds) from the state is unknown.

A breakdown of tentative Federal cost estimates is as follows:

Physical Improvements

    Visitor Center and Headquarters, Interpretive
    Facilities, Campgrounds and Campsites, Canoe
    Launching Facilities, Employee Residences,
    Ranger Stations, Maintenance Buildings,
    Roads and Trails

Total Development	$2,850,000
Real Property Acquisition	$4,600,000
Total Capital Outlay	$7,450,000
Management and Protection	$ 287,505
Annual Operation and Maintenance	$ 100,000

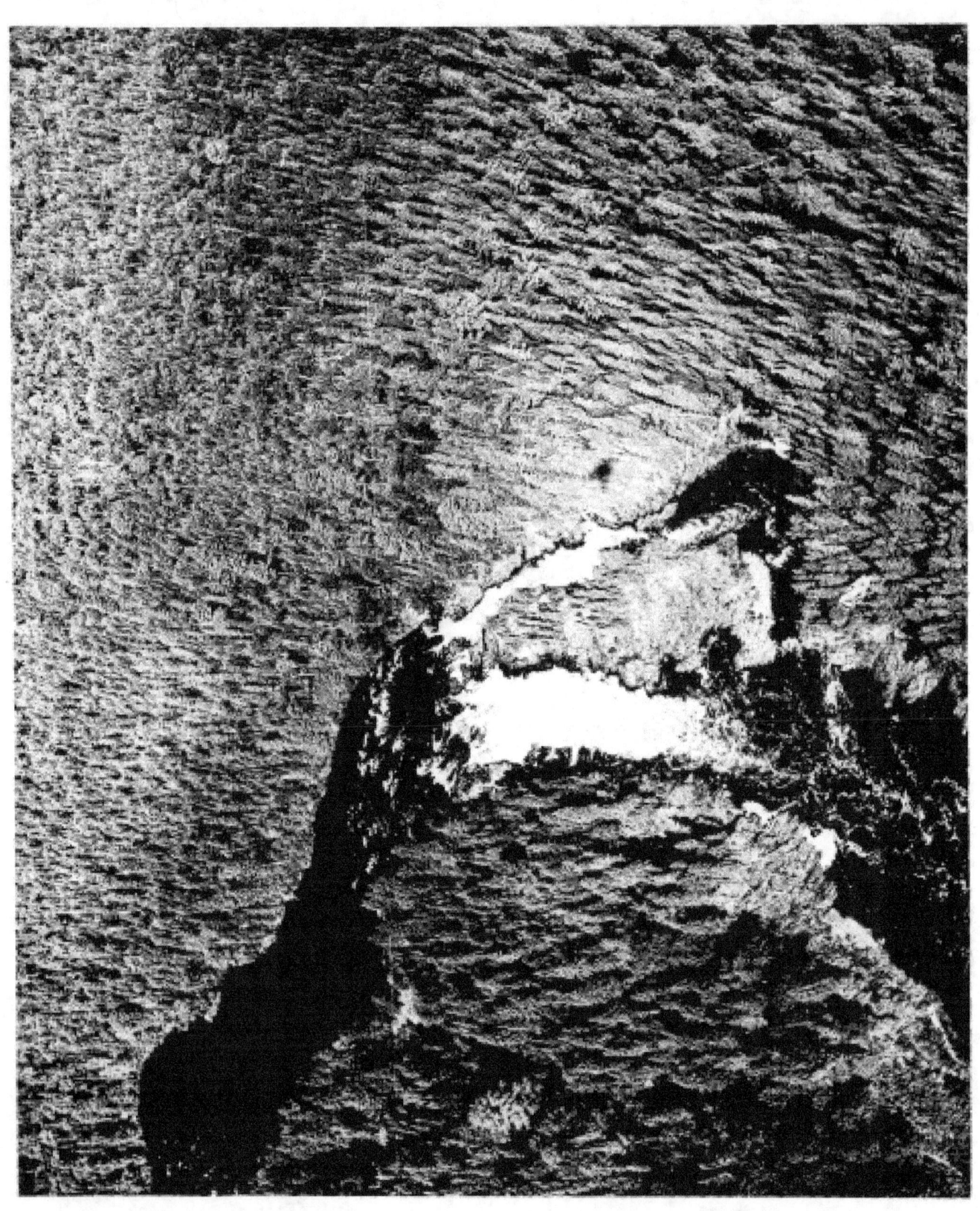

Maine Forest Service
Illus. 5. Allagash Falls

Maine Forest Service
Illus. 6. Portage around Allagash Falls.

STATE OF MAINE

————

In the Year of Our Lord Nineteen Hundred
Sixty-three

————

S.P. 581--L.D. 1534

AN ACT Creating an Allagash River Authority for State of Maine.

————

Be it enacted by the People of the State of Maine, as follows:

Sec. 1. R. S., c. 35-B, additional. The Revised Statutes are amended
by adding a new chapter 35-B, to read as follows:

'Chapter 35-B

Allagash River Authority.

Sec. 1. Policy. It is declared to be the policy of the State of
Maine to provide for the preservation of the natural beauty and wilderness character of the Allagash River Watercourse while utilizing the
natural economic resources of the watercourse.

Sec. 2. Definitions. The following terms as used in this chapter
are defined as follows:

I. Agreements. "Agreements" includes leases, easements, cooperative
agreements, gifts and options for purchase of land or the development
rights to land.

II. Authority. "Authority" means the Allagash River Authority
established under this chapter.

III. Development rights. "Development rights" means the right to
construct buildings or improvements on land and the right to lease
such constructed buildings or improvements to any person, corporation

or governmental authority. The term shall not be applied to prohibit the cutting and harvesting of timber or removal of minerals and shall not be applied to restrict the exercise of those rights commonly known as flowage and driving rights as they may now exist.

Sec. 3. Allagash River Authority. There is created the Allagash River Authority to administer this chapter. The authority shall consist of 5 members, viz: The Forest Commissioner, the Director of State Parks and Recreation, the Commissioner of Inland Fisheries and Game, the Director of the School of Forestry at the University of Maine and the Attorney General. The members of the authority shall elect a chairman who shall preside at all meetings of the authority when present. The authority shall meet as often as necessary, at such times and places as the chairman may designate. Any 3 members shall constitute a quorum for the transaction of the business of the authority. The Forestry Department, State Park and Recreation Commission, Department of Inland Fisheries and Game and Department of Attorney General shall cooperate with the authority in the administration of its duties. The members of the authority shall serve without compensation.

Sec. 4. Allagash Advisory Committee. An advisory committee consisting of 7 members shall be appointed by the Governor, with the advice and consent of the Council, who shall serve until the termination of the authority. A vacancy shall be filled for the unexpired term in the same manner in which a regular appointment is made. The members of the advisory committee shall receive no compensation for their services.

The advisory committee shall meet upon the call of the chairman of the authority. The committee shall render to the authority information and advice concerning the administration of the authority.

Sec. 5. Duties of the authority. The authority shall formulate plans and proposals for preserving the Allagash River Watercourse so that the people of the State and its visitors may be assured of the continued opportunity to enjoy the benefits of the Allagash River Watercourse as a place of natural interest and scenic beauty. The duties and functions of the authority shall include, but not be restricted to, the following:

I. Examination. Examine the Allagash River Watercourse in order to determine those features that should be preserved.

II. Negotiation. Negotiate tentative agreements between the landowners along the Allagash River Watercourse and the State of Maine to assure people of the continued opportunity to enjoy the benefits and scenic beauty of the Allagash.

III. Consultation. Consult with and seek the advice of conservation and naturalist groups in the planning and development of the watercourse.

IV. Rules and standards. Formulate rules and standards for the use, maintenance and operation of the Allagash River Watercourse.

Sec. 6. Tentative agreements. The authority, in the name of the State, shall enter into tentative agreements with the landowners in respect to lands, interest in land, leases, cooperative agreements, agreements and development rights, consistent with the policy and provisions of this chapter. Tentative agreements shall be entered into under such terms and subject to such conditions and restrictions as the authority, after consultation with the advisory committee, may determine.

Sec. 7. Approval by Legislature. The plans, proposal, rules and standards for the use, maintenance and operation of the Allagash River Watercourse and the tentative agreements shall all be subject to the final approval of the 102nd Legislature or subject to the approval of any prior special session of the 101st Legislature.

Sec. 8. Construction. Nothing in this chapter shall be construed to impair the authority of any public body, heretofore or hereafter created by the Legislature, in the exercise of the powers granted to any such public body.'

Sec. 2. Expiration date. In the event the 102nd Legislature, or the 101st Legislature meeting in special session, shall not take action to approve the tentative agreements referred to in this act, then this act shall terminate June 30, 1965, unless otherwise extended by legislative action.

APPENDIX B

RELATIONSHIP OF THE PROPOSED ALLAGASH NATIONAL RIVERWAY TO RECREATION
ADVISORY COUNCIL POLICY CIRCULAR NO. 1 "FEDERAL EXECUTIVE BRANCH
POLICY GOVERNING THE SELECTION, ESTABLISHMENT, AND ADMINISTRATION
OF NATIONAL RECREATION AREAS"   Of March 26, 1963

A review of data contained in this report reveals that the proposed
Allagash National Riverway meets the primary criteria governing selection, establishment, and administration of natural recreation areas as
defined in the Recreation Advisory Council Circular No. 1 as follows:

Spacious Area. The Allagash National Riverway is a spacious area,
including within its perimeter an aggregate gross area of approximately
192,000 acres of land and water surface. In the heart of Maine's backwoods the Allagash River flows northward for nearly 100 miles through
uplands of unbroken forest. The suggested boundary for this river and
lake area would encompass the principal waterway travel routes, typically adapted to canoes and considered to have primitive recreation
qualities and importance to overall preservation objectives.

Carrying Capacity in Relation to Type of Recreation Served. The
Allagash National Riverway would be located and designed to achieve a
comparatively high recreation carrying capacity, in relation to the
type of recreation primarily to be served. Studies to determine the
recreational carrying capacity are essential to ensure that the enjoyment of future users will not be jeopardized by severe overcrowding
that would bring about deterioration and eventual destruction of area
features and atmosphere. Primitive water travel in this river and

lake area takes precedence over all other recreation use. Travel and camping on portions of the river and many of the lakes are a challenge and are appropriate to a dispersed and rustic type of recreation rather than to a concentrated, intense type of use.

Significant Recreation Opportunity. The Allagash National River-way would provide recreation opportunities significant enough to assure interstate patronage. A host of out-of-state persons seek pleasure in the State of Maine annually. Preserving the Allagash in its free-flowing state and perpetuating a primitive recreation experience will strengthen the image of a State already famous for its northwoods atmosphere and rugged features.

Requires Federal Involvement. Preservation and enhancement of the recreation values are dependent upon the interrelationship of the Allagash waterways and the forested watershed. This relationship calls for sound management, coordinated planning, and development by the Federal Government in cooperation with the State, Counties, and private landowners. Investment costs are estimated at about $7,000,000.

The principal purpose of the administering agency will be to insure the quality of the recreation experience by maintaining the physical quality of the river, lakes, and tributaries, the water quantity there-in, and the primitive northwoods environment, and by encouraging wise management practices of the renewable resources throughout the entire watershed. The establishment of a National Riverway, based on policies governing the selection, establishment, and administration of National

2

Recreation Areas would be a logical way to obtain these desired objectives. It would give national recognition to a high quality recreation experience, and to the significance of the unique, natural, and semi-wild quality of the Allagash waterways and the environment through which these waters flow.

Location in Relation to Urban Areas. The area under consideration is nonurban in character. The population within a radius of 250 miles (Canada excluded) is approximately 1.7 million or about 33.5 persons per square mile. There are three major cities within this zone of influence; Portland, Maine in the United States and Quebec and Montreal in Canada.

The general area is served by U.S. Highway 2, Maine State Highway 11, and Province of Quebec Highway 24. Locally, the area is served by private logging roads which are used by the general public. These roads are generally open except during the winter season when snow and ice prevent travel by automobile. Access under these conditions, of course, would be restricted to specialized transportation means.

Primary Purpose. Outdoor recreation would be the primary purpose of the Allagash National Riverway--to insure that present and future generations can continue to have a primitive northwoods canoeing experience in an eastern United States area that affords sufficient size and quality. In order to achieve this purpose, it is necessary to protect the natural free-flowing character of the river and the primitive northwoods flavor of its surroundings.

Deficient Public Recreation Opportunities. The recreation area
under consideration is located in a region where other current and
planned programs (Federal and non-Federal) will not fulfill high priority
recreation needs in the foreseeable future. Baxter State Park would
adjoin the Allagash National Riverway on the southeast. One additional
state park - Aroostook - exists in the northern half of Maine.

Secondary criteria for selection of national recreation areas
are fulfilled by the area under consideration, as follows:

Location in Relation to High Population Densities. The proposed
Allagash National Riverway is located within 285 miles of the metro-
politan area of Boston and within 450 miles of New York City, hub of
the densely populated Middle Atlantic U.S. Census Division. Furthermore, the area under consideration is in an area which has a comparatively low amount of Federally provided recreation carrying capacity.

Scarce or Disappearing Resources. The Allagash River is one of
the few remaining major free-flowing streams in the eastern United
States. This river, if properly protected, will provide a high quality
recreation environment that is gradually disappearing from our national
scene.

Compatibility with Recreation Potential of Adjacent Rural Areas
in Private Ownership. Dedication of the Allagash National Riverway
to a more subdued type of conservation principle will complement the
recreation habits of Maine's citizens or the host of out-of-State
persons who seek pleasure in the State.

4

Located Within a Redevelopment Area. The Allagash River largely lies in Aroostook County which is designated as a (5b) redevelopment area under the Area Redevelopment Act (Public Law 87-27).

Recommendation. It is recommended that favorable consideration be given to the inclusion of the Allagash National Riverway in the system of National Recreation Areas.

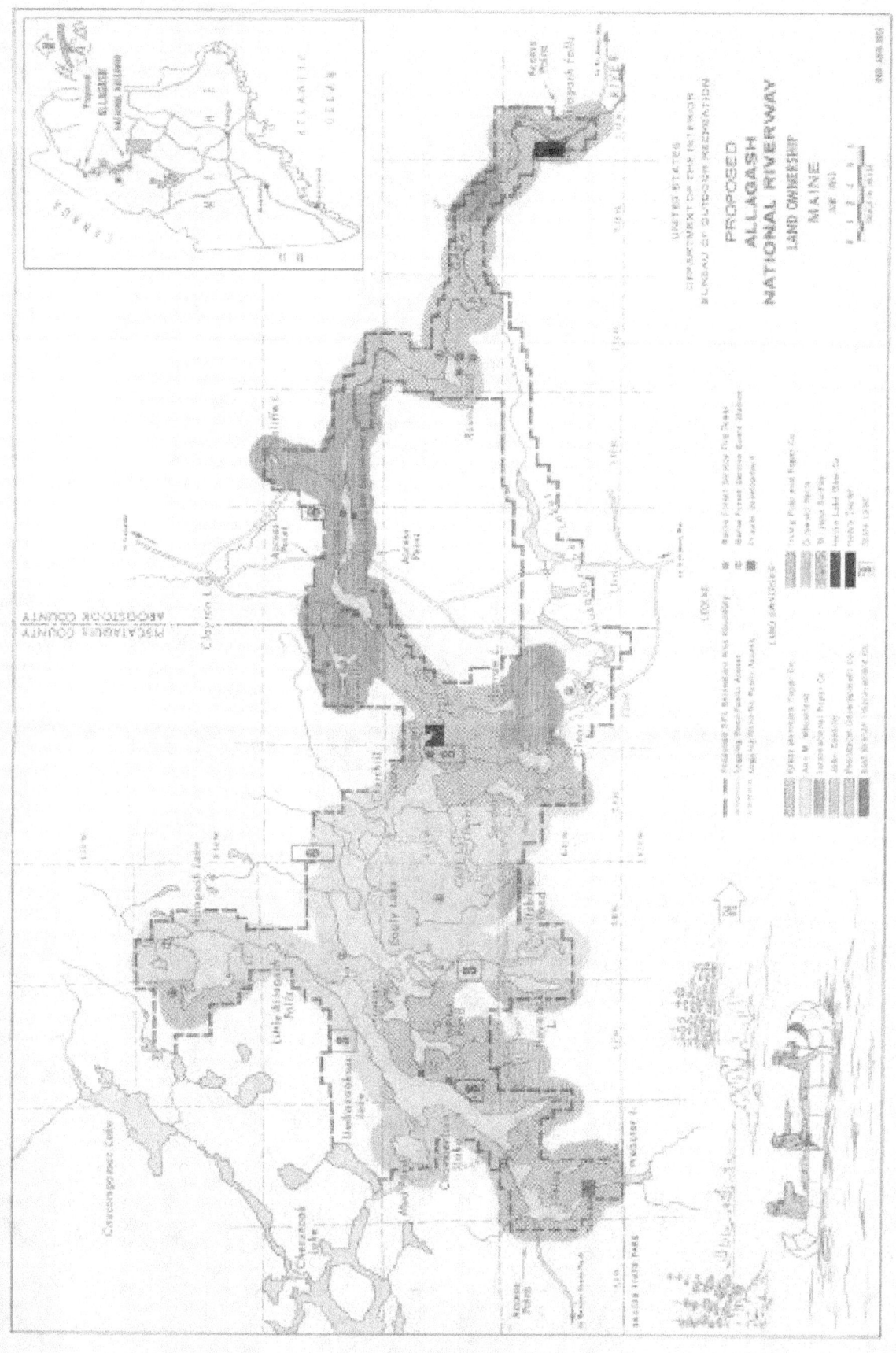

UNITED STATES
DEPARTMENT OF THE INTERIOR
BUREAU OF OUTDOOR RECREATION

PROPOSED
ALLAGASH
NATIONAL RIVERWAY
LAND OWNERSHIP
MAINE

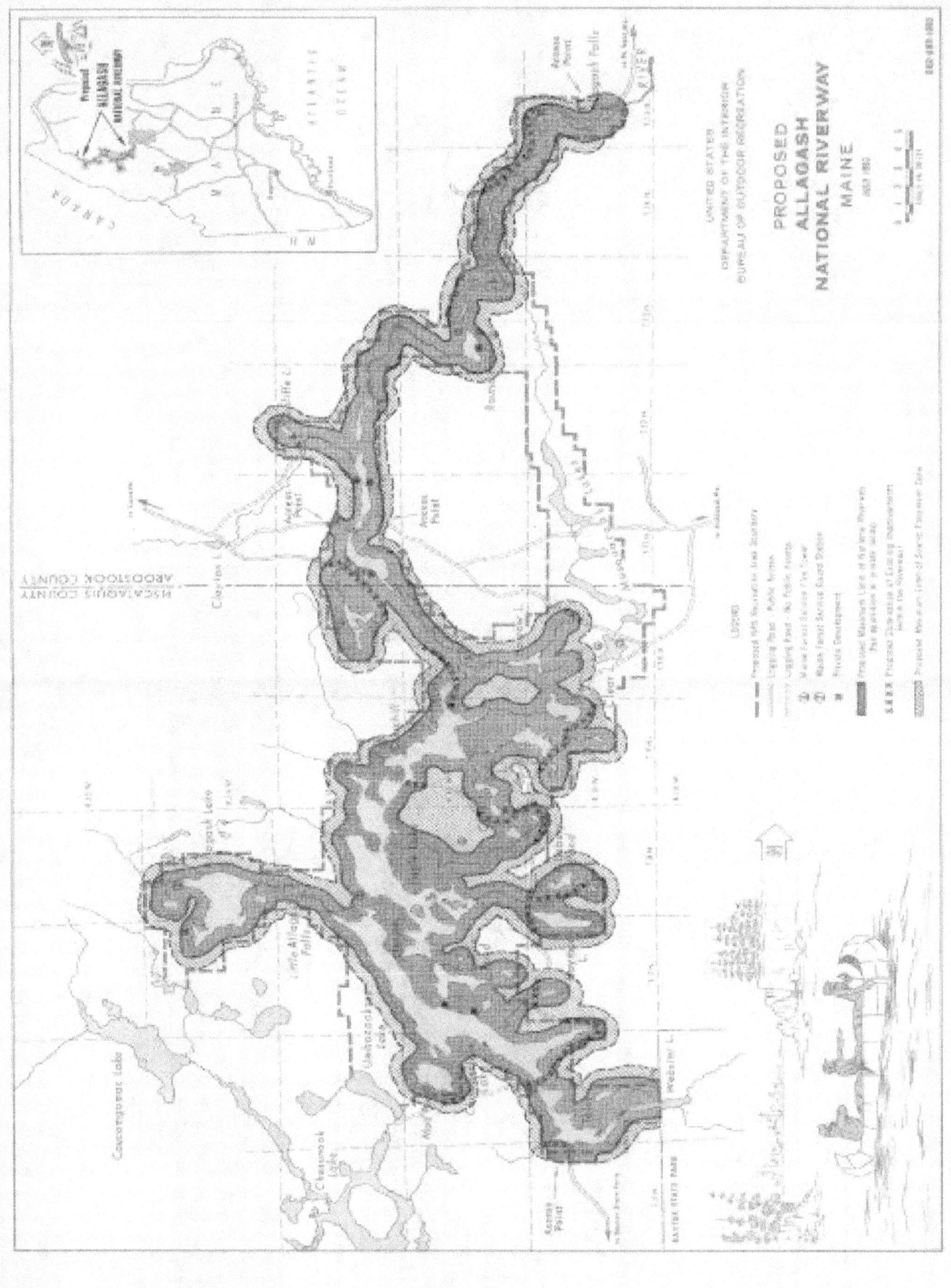

UNITED STATES
DEPARTMENT OF THE INTERIOR
BUREAU OF OUTDOOR RECREATION

PROPOSED
ALLAGASH
NATIONAL RIVERWAY
MAINE